GLIMPSES of OLD PA

by Ernest Ryman and Geoffrey Mead

Contents

Introduction

Though forerunners had made use of 'Celtic' fields on the slopes to the north of Ladies Mile Road, Old Patcham sat for centuries like an egg, snug in a nest of surrounding hills. Its chief features were the church, farm and mill on a ridge of higher ground above the Wellesbourne stream. That ridge can still be followed by a footpath starting opposite Court Farm, running alongside the churchyard into Highview Avenue (north and south), dog-legging past the First School and the former mill cottages to connect with a rough path down to the Old London Road.

However snug, Patcham was not cosily dry. Indeed its name may well derive from the Old English *Peece* or *Pacce* (pronounced 'Patch'), meaning watery, miry or splashy. Such a derivation would not be surprising because the former spring and pond by the church merely contributed to a stronger flow at the foot of Church Hill, where water from the main Waterhall springs was already in lively motion.

The Domesday survey showed Patcham to be much larger than Brighton and more heavily populated. Its taxable value was correspondingly greater, too. At that time the parish included Hollingbury, Moulsecoomb, Withdean and Tongdean, all of which became part of Brighton in 1927, except for Tongdean which was transferred to Hove.

Until the middle of the last century, the village was almost entirely concerned with agriculture, but with the growth of Brighton and a decline in farming, an increasing proportion of its population found other employment in Brighton and in market-garden activity. Greater changes came after the 1920s with increased urban development of both single dwellings and planned 'Garden City' estates, which brought a profusion of housing styles to the village surrounds.

It is hoped that this collection of scenes in Patcham 1900-1940 may increase a sense of local identity in residents and whet the appetites of at least a few to know more. The past is ours. It belongs to us; and has something to tell us.

Picture 1: Lying in a prominent position above the heart of the old village, the church of All Saints has a history dating back to Saxon times. Parts of the present building were erected as early as the 12th C. One can but envy earlier churchgoers their approach along the raised footpath by the churchyard wall, with the pond alongside. The spring which fed the pond was one of several forming the source of the Wellesbourne. Today wedding-groups pose for photographs where ducks once swam, and farm horses drank their fill. (circa 1900)

Picture 2: This view (c. 1910) of the other side of the pond gives a comprehensive idea of Court Farm buildings, indicating the farm's importance in the agricultural life of the village. Its name reveals that local justice was dispensed on this site, and the size of the barns underlines the scope of its harvests. Since 1925 the farm's 733 acres have belonged to Brighton Corporation. Previously it had been the property of the Marquess of Abergavenny's family continuously from 1439. Faced with knapped flints, the farmhouse in Vale Avenue was first built in the seventeenth century and is a 'listed' building.

Picture 3: Even more impressive is the farm's magnificent dovecote, whose walls are castle-thick with flint and contain 550 nesting-boxes (or potences). At least 300 years old, it is claimed to be Brighton's only scheduled 'ancient monument'. Dovecotes were familiar mediaeval sights, providing welcome variety of fare, especially during the winter months when salted meat or fish became monotonous. However, peasants detested the doves, being allowed neither to own the birds nor kill them, even when they fed voraciously off the villagers' own crops. This photograph was taken c. 1900.

Picture 4: (c. 1930) Moving down Church Hill (on the right above), one reaches this junction with both the Old and New London Road, a very open corner now dominated by the Black Lion and Patcham Fountain. The large hotel was erected in 1929, replacing an earlier villa. Until then the Black Lion had been further along the Old London Road (see Picture 6), where Jon's Ale was advertised as the "Cyclist's Drink" twenty years before. The Victoria Fountain remains a favourite stopping place for coaches and buses, both into Brighton and from further afield. The petrol vehicle in the centre replaced an earlier horse-drawn bus service which took passengers to Preston Circus until the outbreak of the First World War.

Picture 5: From the turn of the century into the 1930s, Brightonians would from time to time emerge from their urban setting to enjoy the rural atmosphere of villages like Patcham, especially when there was a pond with ducks as an added attraction. Saddlescombe, Falmer and Rottingdean, as well as Patcham, provided such a setting and all four offered in addition modestly priced refreshment in at least one Tea Garden. "Ye Olde Cottage" at Patcham used an intriguing variety of garden furniture, and a parrot (centre). In unkind weather tea was served indoors with an even more interesting range of wooden beams, sideboards, tables and rural paraphernalia.

Picture 6: Turning south into the Old London Road, one soon reaches the establishment of J. Harris & Son, which not only provided Patcham's Postal Telegram Service but also served as a bakery and corn-merchant's. The remarkable Joseph Harris started the bakery c. 1875 and built the windmill above Waterhall five years later. The Post Office remains in the hands of the Harris family to this day, in contrast with its foreground neighbour, the original "Black Lion", now quietly relaxing as 110-112, Old London Road. Though painted over, the Hotel Signboard is still there today.

Picture 7: Stepping back from the heart of Patcham, one has a view here of Church Hill winding its way up to the top of the ridge on the left, with Harris's Post Office helping to locate the Old London Road on the right. At this time, in early 1920s, the village lay astride the busy London Road and had assumed 'highway functions', providing initially a blacksmith's, Inn and Horse dealer, and by the 1920s tea-gardens, garage and roadhouse. Gradually the traffic proved too great and the London Road by-pass was opened in 1926. This photograph was taken from the grassy slopes where the main London Road runs today.

Picture 8: This 1920 photograph was taken south of the village, from a position close to Ballard's mill. Patcham Place lies in the trees (middle left) and the chimneys of Church Hill cottages can be seen below the right-hand skyline. The barn on the extreme right was part of Patcham Place Farm and on its left is Elms Farm now the Elms shopping centre at the foot of Ladies Mile Road. By the inter-war period farming was at an all-time low and the big Patcham estates of the Kemp family and the Abergavennys were put on the market, enabling hundreds of acres to be bought by developers for the creation of Brighton's suburbs. A glimpse of school playground activity can be seen on the extreme left, alongside a house which marks the beginning of a developing trend.

Picture 9: In this view of Court Farm in 1928 there is nothing to suggest that the village has yet been absorbed into Greater Brighton. A brave ladder stands against a good, old-fashioned hayrick, with a fine Sussex wagon standing by. The Great Barn behind continued in use into the 1980s when it at last succumbed to conversion, providing housing units and a community hall. Though the massive barn indicates the scale of corn and fleeces which had once brought prosperity, the Depression reveals itself in the state of the sheds. A primitive water-supply system can be seen in the phased, diagonal guttering running across the length of the roof of the shed before passing through a stone gutter and into the brick trough.

Picture 10: The photographer here is looking up Vale Avenue eastwards. The flint building on the right is Court farmhouse, with the farmsheds, barn, pond and dovecote out of the picture to the right. In the centre of the picture on the left-hand side of the road, are two semi-detached homes which are still standing: and though not visible here there is a monogram A above the door under the central gable, indicating the name of the estate owners, the Abergavennys, who also arranged for the date 1909 to be displayed with glass marbles. Such new housing for farm-workers was a rare commodity in that period of agricultural depression.

Picture 11: Patcham Place has been a mansion since 1558, but what is seen here is a rebuilding for John Paine in 1764, with a striking facade incorporating black mathematical tiles. This finely balanced edifice remains a delight to the eye not only by the manner in which the whole site is maintained by Brighton Corporation but also because, back in the middle of the last century, the then owner, Major Paine, refused to allow the railway to pass through his land by a cutting - hence the nearby tunnel. In the same spirit, a terrier on the left keeps a wary gaze on the intruding camera.

Picture 12: This picture has been included to give a close-up view of both the building and a group of people who evoke the atmosphere of pre-First-World-War England at a particular level. The simple, well-proportioned facade of the house provides an apt frame for the modest elegance of the porch, while varied comfortable clothing protects the assembled company as the uniformed maid on the right brings out the stirrup cup. The house itself has been used as a Youth Hostel since 1939, after accommodating several classes of Patcham Junior children in the mid 1930s.

Picture 13: Tucked away behind the Old London Road, in a cosy time-capsule, these 18th C. cottages form part of an enclosed area with a pair of two-roomed bungalows out of picture on the left-hand side opposite. Surprisingly, this view has changed but little and with tiny front gardens the Square has an almost urban atmosphere. The use of flint and brick was common in the Downs. Flints, having usually been cleared from the fields by pauper labour, became the building stone for cottage and manor-house alike. The bricks possibly came from the coastal brickfields in Brighton and would have reached Patcham as a 'back cargo' on the carts of market-gardeners and corn-dealers.

Picture 14: This view of flint and clay-tile cottages has a timeless quality taking us back to the England observed by Hardy and Cobbett. However such thoughts need to be tempered with the realisation that the setting for Cold Comfort Farm lay just a few miles away. Sheep-hurdles leaning against the hedge indicate a pastoral economy, and drying washing on the bushes was by no means uncommon: prints of 19th C. Brighton show commercial laundries drying clothes in a similar fashion. Standean takes its name from the sarsen stones that lay in the valley bottom, sharing the same Saxon root as Stanmer and the Steine in Brighton.

Picture 15: Known today as Ladies Mile Road, the Drove was formerly a route for farm animals between Patcham and Stanmer. These cottages still survive at the western end of the shopping parade there. In the mid-distance is a barn (then part of Place Farm) which became the Barn Methodist Church. In 1910 the tenants still had names that were familiar throughout Sussex - Allfrey, Norman and Trangmar. Downland villages generally had few cottages, often tied to the jobs of the agricultural estate-workers, and as the work-force shrank with increasing mechanisation some housing was demolished on many estates, leaving a number of 20th C. villages smaller than their predecessors.

Picture 16: This view, c. 1928, is of the same road but looking south-west, from high up the hill. It was still known as the Droveway then and its muddy state suggests that perhaps animals were still driven along it. Being a major ownership boundary, separating Abergavenny and Kemp land, the road was always likely to contain different building styles on either side. This variety was further ensured by the splitting up into separate plotlands, with no overall control of design. These homes are the result of a 1921 landsale. Mrs Elms, who provided this photograph, lived with her parents in the second home from the left and enjoyed a glorious view over Eastwick Bottom, which became almost filled with the Ladies Mile Estate within four years.

Picture 17: This scene in 1932 shows the north side of Ladies Mile Road and a greater harmony of house-design which became possible with the sale of larger plots. Pavements and verges have appeared as part of the overall provision, together with telegraph poles, yet a horse-drawn cart still competes with the petrol-engine and a tricycle cart stands purposefully in a working position. In the middle distance on the left only the corner house stands in Highview Avenue South and the parade of shops below the cottages has yet to appear. The Ladies Mile Estate was the brainchild of George Ferguson who designed the project on garden-city lines with lots of open spaces and all-electric power in the homes.

Picture 18: Everything is very much under control in the 1938 classroom at Patcham Junior School, with well-disciplined rows of desks and fixed seating, acquired with the opening of the new school the previous year, following a decade of overcrowding associated with the development of the Ladies Mile Estate. Patcham's original National School had opened in the Old London Road c. 1862, in buildings which still serve as part of the Special School there. During the 1930s substantial use had to be made of both Patcham Place and Mackie Hall, with less than half the pupils being taught in the old school. Many Patcham residents have developed a deep-rooted attachment to the area and one wonders how many of Class 3 still live in the area only recently colonised by their families in 1938.

Picture 19: In 1939 Brighton was thought to provide a safe war-haven for London schoolchildren, and this revealing photograph tells its own story of recently arrived evacuees, slightly crumpled but not without the odd brave smile for the camera. Each person was provided with a gas-mask in a cardboard box, of the kind correctly slung round the neck of the boy sitting on the bottom right-hand step. Apart from that item youngsters carried the rest of their personal belongings in a brown-paper carrier bag. Underground air-raid shelters were provided, in which all the older children sheltered, sometimes for two or three hours. The youngest pupils went into concrete shelters in the playground.

Picture 20: This open view of the southern half of Patcham in 1916 shows an area now almost totally covered with houses. There remain just a few surviving buildings to help contemporary recognition - an isolated pair of cottages at the crossroads in the middle distance still stand today on the corner of Greenfield Crescent and Braybon Avenue. Below these lie two separate villas, the Grange and Ashburnham Lodge, forerunners of the major urban growth. Neighbouring each were market gardens, helping to compensate for the agricultural slump. The National School can be seen in the foreground, with the Old London Road running along behind it.

Picture 21: This military camp is pitched on land belonging to Place Farm, and the foreground is currently part of Highview Avenue North. In the distance are the hills of the Chichester Estate and the trees of Stanmer Park. On the right-hand skyline stand some of the first homes that were built on Drove Road (later Ladies Mile Road) after 1921, when the Abergavenny Estate was sold and broken up. Behind the tents are the lands of the Kemp Estate, owners of Patcham Place. This area was sold off in 1931 up to the long hedge under the left-hand skyline. George Ferguson built the Ladies Mile estate from 1931-34, and later extended into Abergavenny land behind the hedge.

Picture 22: Though all the buildings in this scene have now been demolished and even the road-angle smoothed, the London Road can be seen here in a sedate period, at its junction with Tongdean Lane. The flint buildings, trees and horses suggest a rural atmosphere but gas-lamps and telegraph-poles tell of the road's suburban role between Brighton and Patcham. Tea and Strawberry Gardens boosted the local economy which also benefitted from the town's need for fresh food - the Jersey Dairy Farm of Mr Tebay and Marshall's Withdean Nursery exemplify this fact. The area was also a great supplier of hay until the trade was affected by the car-boom of the 1930s.

Picture 23: This tree-lined approach to Brighton was already attractive at the very beginning of this century, when the pace of the horse-drawn bus pleasantly reflected the dignity of the villas. Yet for centuries this was not the usual route between Brighton and London. Preferred journeys reached the metropolis via Lewes, or along the Dyke Road via Saddlescombe and Henfield. However, after becoming a Turnpike Road in 1770, it eventually served as the main London Road when a new road opened between Pyecombe and Bolney in 1810. The villas on the right, "Devonia" and "Heron's Court" survived until the late 1980s, but the hedge and trees had succumbed to an earlier road-widening scheme at the junction of London Road with Carden Avenue.

Picture 24: This was Ballard's Mill, built towards the end of the 18th C. and only taken down around 1900. The Mill House remains today and a small rose garden opposite the large rustic garden gate marks the actual site of the mill itself. Earlier mills, including one in the 16th C., probably stood in the same position, each one as dominant a feature of Patcham as the Parish Church at the other end of the ridge. Ballard also owned a bakery, lower down near the London Road, reached by a footpath known as the Pilgrims' Way. Baking bread for Brighton was sufficiently profitable for Joseph Harris to set up his rival bakery in the Old London Road and subsequently build his own mill above Waterhall, as can be seen in the next two pictures.

Picture 25: This photograph was taken c. 1929 from the upper reaches of the Waterhall valley, below Patcham mill. Today the same scene is dominated by the new by-pass, but then Mill Road itself was only a mere track running up the sides of Coney and Red Hills. The nearby golf-course was privately owned until Brighton Corporation acquired it in 1936, as part of the West Blatchington Estate. In extending the nine-hole course in 1934 it is alleged that the owner absorbed a nudist camp near the seventh green. Patcham's large Parish area included a number of isolated hamlets, such as Moulsecoomb, Standean and Waterhall, as well as the central village community.

Picture 26: Waterhall Mill was one of the last mills to be built in Sussex. Today it is more usually referred to as Patcham Mill, though residents of Westdene regard it with affection as being theirs. A forty-foot tower Mill, erected in 1884/5 by Joseph Harris (see **Picture 6**), it ceased to grind corn in 1924. By 1936 the Mill had been converted into a home and, with its commanding views it is not surprising that it was taken over by the Forces during World War II, when it was used by the Home Guard.

Picture 27: The Robin Hood Garage was a typical part of inter-war ribbon-development along the London Road approach to Brighton and somehow this scene captures all the energy and confusion of the period. Each building has a different shape; signs proliferate; a purposeless ladder masks a tubbed shrub and a sprawl of unwanted, defunct material litters the side wall. Yet the vehicles are full of character and no-one can dispute the wisdom of the modest sign, "DRIVE CAUTIOUSLY". As late as 1937 the Council for the Preservation of Rural England protested; ..."ancient buildings are being constantly converted into garages or petrol stations and rendered needlessly hideous by a medley of advertisements".

Picture 28: Providing a contrast with the last scene, the Chattri commemorates Indian troops who died during the Great War. It takes the form of a Ghat, an Indian riverside landing stairway, traditionally associated with memorials to the dead. It was designed by a young Hindu architect, constructed of Sicilian marble and unveiled by the Prince of Wales. Its cost was shared between the India Office and Brighton Corporation. Architect, E.C. Henriques, also designed the south gate of the Royal Pavilion which was presented by the people of India to the people of Brighton later in the same year. The memorial is said to sit well on its downland slope above Standean valley, carrying a tranquil air that seems to complement the very English nature of Downland.

Epilogue

A glimpse in words, from a statement produced in the early 1920s by the longest serving headteacher of Patcham Board School, Richard Phillips, 1884-1920

. . .Members of the Board included the Vicar, Mr Friend (grocer), Mr Harris (baker and mill-owner), Daniel Hack, J.P. (Quaker resident) and Mr Keen (gentleman farmer). The school roll was approximately 100, of whom some came from the heart of the village itself, including the Square, Church Hill, Pond Cottages and the Drove. A considerable number however also attended from Withdean, including the children of coachmen, gardeners and butlers who resided on the small estates of commuters using Preston Park Station for London trains. . . Outlying hamlets at Waterhall and Standean Nursery Gardens at Dyke Road meant long distances for pupils to walk daily. Parents included shepherds, cowmen, ploughmen, gamekeeper, blacksmith, sexton, railwaymen and roadmen. . .

. . .With a large meadow to the north (now "Meadowside") and open fields on both east and west, farm cultivation provided varied interests. Oxen drawing the plough would stop at the end of a furrow and eat the shoots of blackcurrant bushes from the headmaster's garden. Partridges collected in coveys at dusk and a fox crossed the premises. May Day was observed by a procession of scholars carrying garlands around the parish. . .

Main Sources

Bennett, H.S.	*"Life on the English Manor 1150-1400"*	Cambridge University Press	1948
Brandon, P. & Short, B.	*"The South East of England from 1000 A.D."*	Longman	1990
Brighton Reference Library			1920s
Brighton and Hove Gazette			1930s
Carder, T.	*"The Encyclopaedia of Brighton"*	East Sussex County Libraries	1990
Carter, R. & Travis, A. and 4th-year pupils at Patcham Junior School	*"Patcham Junior School Golden Jubilee"*	Lewis Cohen Urban Studies Centre	1987
East Sussex Record Office	*"Abergavenny Estate Papers"*		various dates
Farrant, S.	*"Changes in Brighton & Hove Suburbs: Preston and Patcham 1841-1871"*	Farrant, S.	1985
Pike's and Kelly's Directories			various dates

Other Dyke Publications

"Guide to the Devil's Dyke" (1984)
  Second Edition (1988)

"Views & Legend of the Devil's Dyke" (1984)
  Second Reprint (1987)
  Third Reprint (1990)

"Rottingdean in Old Picture Postcards" (1985)
  Second Edition (1990)

"Devil's Dyke in Old Picture Postcards" (1989)

"Glimpses of Old Edmonton" (March 1992)
  Second Edition (May 1992)

Published by Dyke Publications
38 Bankside, Brighton BN1 5GN

Printed by Carmichael Printers & Co Ltd
54 Hollingdean Road, Brighton,
Sussex BN2 4AA